34115162

The
Butterfly

Copyright © 1997 Steck-Vaughn Company

Published by Raintree Steck-Vaughn Publishers, an imprint of Steck-Vaughn Company.

Acknowledgments
Project Editor: Helene Resky
Design Manager: Joyce Spicer
Consulting Editor: Kim Merlino
Consultant: Michael Chinery
Illustrated by Stuart Lafford
Designed by Ian Winton and Steve Prosser
Electronic Cover Production: Alan Klemp
Additional Electronic Production: Bo McKinney and Scott Melcer
Photography credits on page 32

Planned and produced by The Creative Publishing Company

Library of Congress Cataloging-in-Publication Data
    Crewe, Sabrina
    The butterfly / Sabrina Crewe ; [illustrated by Stuart Lafford].
        p.   cm. — (Life cycles)
    Includes index.
    Summary: Describes the habitat, food, and life cycle of the monarch butterfly.
    ISBN 0-8172-4364-X (hardcover). — ISBN 0-8172-6227-X (pbk.)
    1. Butterflies — Juvenile literature.   2. Monarch butterfly — Juvenile literature.
3. Butterflies — Life cycles — Juvenile literature.   4. Monarch butterfly — Life cycles —
Juvenile literature.   [1. Monarch butterfly. 2. Butterflies.]   I. Lafford, Stuart.   II. Title.
III. Series: Crewe, Sabrina. Life cycles.
    QL544.2.C74   1997
    595.78'9 — dc20   96-4844
                                                             CIP   AC

1 2 3 4 5 6 7 8 9 0 LB 00 99 98 97 96
Printed and bound in the United States of America.

Words explained in the glossary appear in
bold the first time they are used in the text.

LIFE CYCLES

The
Butterfly

Sabrina Crewe

RSVP

RAINTREE
STECK-VAUGHN
PUBLISHERS
The Steck-Vaughn Company

Austin, Texas

The eggs are on the leaf.

These are the eggs of a
butterfly. They have been
laid on the leaf of a plant.
The eggs are very tiny.

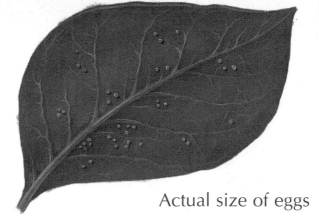

Actual size of eggs

The egg is opening.

Four days have passed. Something
is nibbling through the eggshell. It is
a **caterpillar**.

The caterpillars have hatched.

Actual size of caterpillars

The caterpillars are very small
when they come out of their eggs.
They are eating their eggshells.
This is the caterpillars' first food.

The caterpillar is eating leaves.

The caterpillar grows fast. Now it
has started to feed on plants.

The caterpillar is shedding its skin.

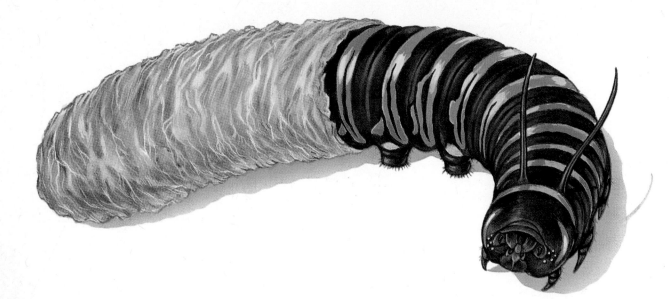

The caterpillar has grown too big for its skin.
The skin splits when it becomes too tight.
Underneath, the caterpillar has a new, looser
skin. Its stripes are very colorful.

The caterpillar has many legs.

The caterpillar uses its ten back legs to move around. The tiny hooks on its legs help the caterpillar hold onto plants. The caterpillar's six front legs help it feed.

The caterpillar is in danger.

The caterpillar has many **predators**.
But its marks warn predators that the
caterpillar tastes bad. This can save
the caterpillar from being eaten.

The caterpillar is fully grown.

The caterpillar is 18 days old.
It has shed its skin four times.
Now the caterpillar fastens its
tail end to a plant.

The caterpillar is changing.

The caterpillar's skin is splitting again. It doesn't look like a caterpillar anymore. The caterpillar is in the **pupa** stage.

Now a **chrysalis** has formed. At first, the skin of the chrysalis is soft, but it soon hardens.

The chrysalis has tiny holes to let air in and out. Inside, the creature is completely changing its shape.

There is a new creature.

This is the chrysalis two weeks later. You can see the creature inside. It is ready to come out.

The chrysalis has split. A butterfly is crawling out! The butterfly has grown wings and **antennae**. Now it has only three pairs of legs.

The butterfly dries its wings.

When the butterfly first appears, its wings are damp and crumpled. When blood pumps into their veins, the wings stretch. Then the butterfly dries its wings in the sunshine.

The butterfly's wings are covered with scales.

The butterfly has two wings on each side of its body. The wings are covered with tiny scales. The scales give the butterfly its beautiful colors. The colors warn predators that the butterfly tastes bad.

17

The butterfly is looking for food.

The butterfly has flown onto a flower. It is feeding on the **nectar** inside the flower. The butterfly collects the nectar with its **proboscis**.

Butterflies love the sunshine.

Butterflies fly mostly on sunny days. They like to live in warm places. When it gets colder in the fall, the butterflies **migrate** to warmer places.

The butterflies have migrated.

The butterflies have flown a long way from their summer home. They have all gathered in the same place. Sometimes the butterflies cover a whole tree!

Spring has come.

The butterflies spend much of the winter asleep on the leaves and branches of trees. When spring comes, the butterflies migrate again. They are leaving their winter home.

The butterflies are ready to mate.

The butterflies have mating smells in their wings. The male and female butterflies find each other by their mating smells.

The female butterfly lays her eggs.

The male and female butterflies have mated to **fertilize** the female's eggs. The female butterfly has found a safe place to lay her eggs. Soon she will fly away and leave the eggs to hatch on their own.

Butterflies need wild places.

Butterflies need places with wildflowers
that have nectar. They need the right
kinds of plants on which to lay their eggs.
People can help butterflies by keeping
wild places safe for them.

Parts of a Butterfly

Wings ———————————————
Covered in tiny, hairy scales

Thorax ———————————————
Middle part of the body

Abdomen ———————————————
Rear part of the body

Butterflies are insects. All insects have three parts to their bodies. These are the head, the **thorax**, and the **abdomen**. All adult insects have six legs. Insects such as butterflies and moths have wings and can fly.

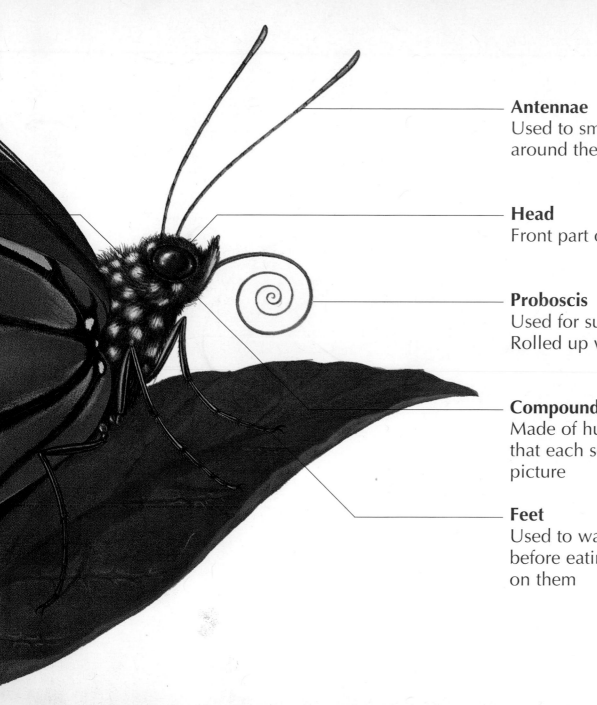

Antennae
Used to smell and sense things around them

Head
Front part of the body

Proboscis
Used for sucking nectar
Rolled up when not feeding

Compound eyes
Made of hundreds of tiny eyes that each see part of the whole picture

Feet
Used to walk and to taste plants before eating them or laying eggs on them

Other Butterflies

The butterfly in this book is a monarch butterfly. Here are some other butterflies from all over the world.

Adonis Blue
Europe

Apollo
Europe

Queen Alexandra's Birdwing
Southeast Asia
The female is the world's largest butterfly.
It can be as big as 11 inches (28 cm) across.

Marbled White
Europe

Long Tailed Skipper
North America

Australian Beak
Australia

Red Admiral
Northern Hemisphere

Eastern Tiger Swallowtail
North America

Where the Monarch Butterfly Lives

Areas where the monarch butterfly lives

Migratory routes of the monarch butterfly

Alaska

CANADA

UNITED STATES

MEXICO

Glossary

Abdomen The rear part of an insect's body

Antennae The feelers on an insect's head used to sense things around them

Caterpillar The larva of a butterfly; the growing stage before it turns into a pupa

Chrysalis The pupa of a butterfly; the stage where it rests and changes into an adult

Fertilize To make a female's eggs able to produce babies

Migrate To move from one place to another when the seasons change

Nectar The sweet liquid made by flowers to attract insects

Predator An animal that hunts and kills other animals for food

Proboscis A tube-shaped mouth used to suck nectar from flowers

Pupa The stage where an insect rests and changes into an adult

Thorax The middle part of an insect's body

Index